spot

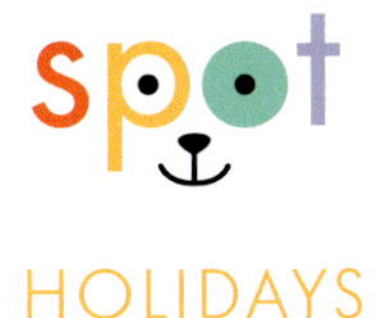

HOLIDAYS

INDEPENDENCE DAY

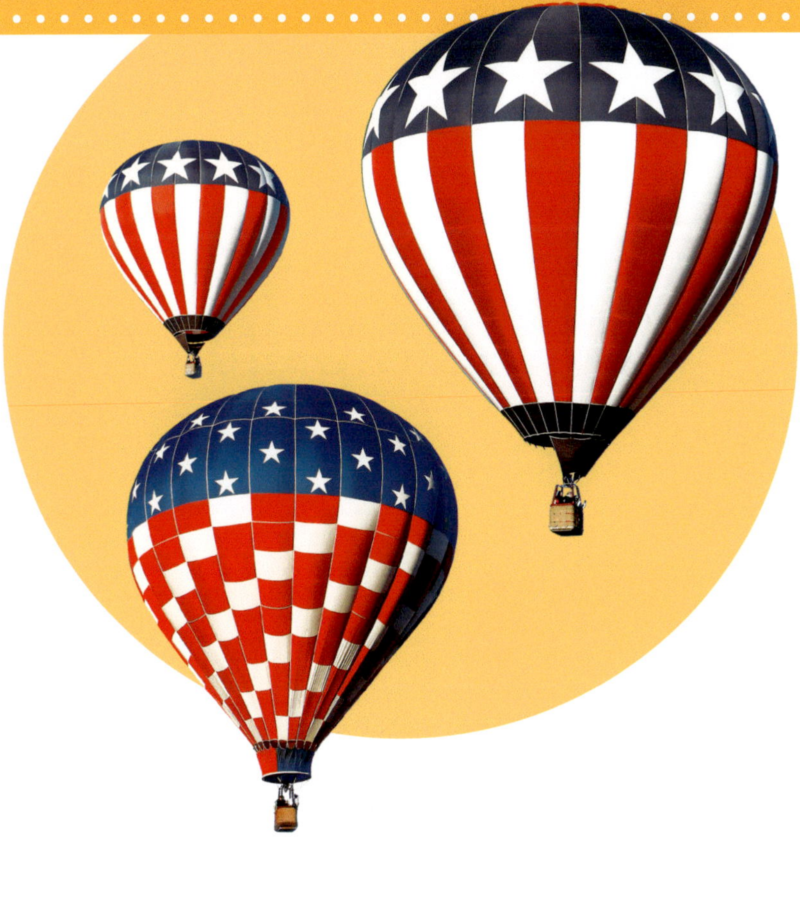

by Mari Schuh

AMICUS | AMICUS INK

band

flag

Look for these words and pictures as you read.

picnic

fireworks

Look at the colors.

It is July 4th.

It is Independence Day!

The United States became a country on July 4, 1776. It is America's birthday!

band

See the band?

It is in a parade.

It plays songs about America.

HS

See the flag?
It is the country's flag.
It has 50 stars and 13 stripes.

flag

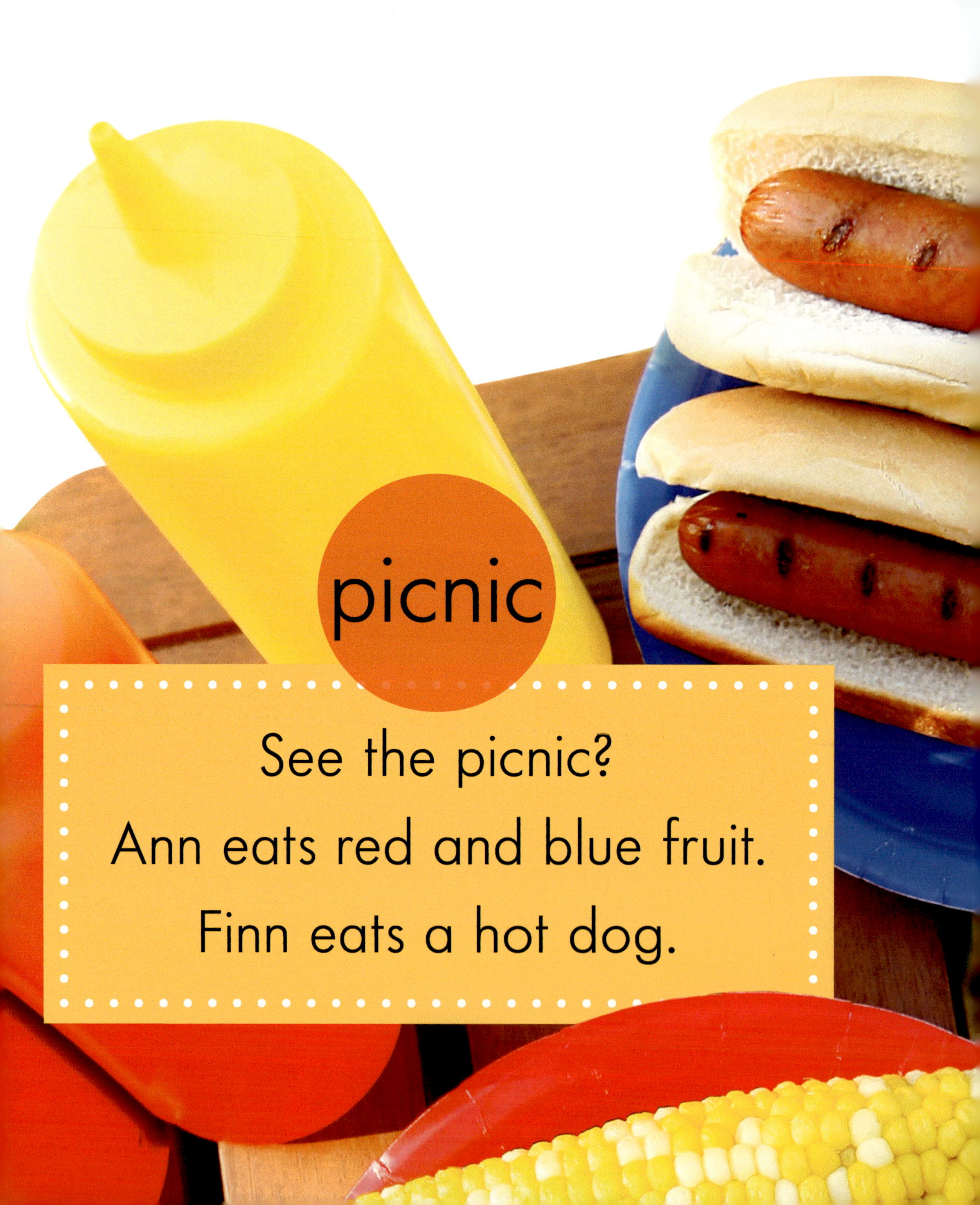

picnic

See the picnic?

Ann eats red and blue fruit.

Finn eats a hot dog.

fireworks

See the fireworks?

Bang!

They are loud and bright.

A family celebrates.
It is a fun day!

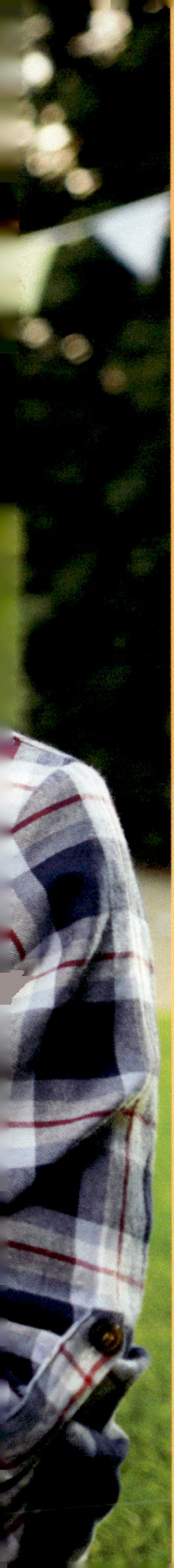

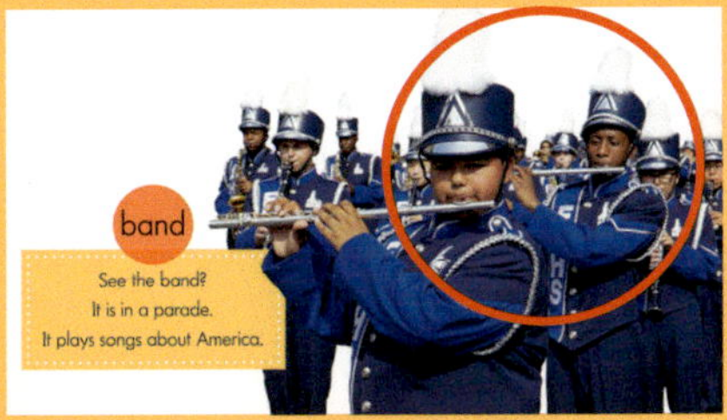

band

See the band?
It is in a parade.
It plays songs about America.

band

flag

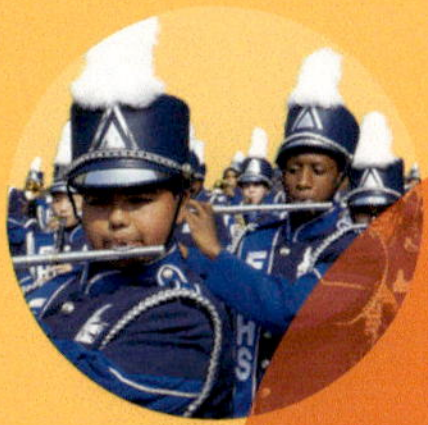

Did you find?

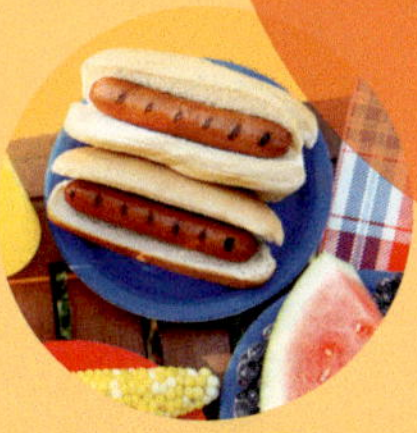

picnic

picnic

See the picnic?
Ann eats red and blue fruit.
Finn eats a hot dog.

fireworks

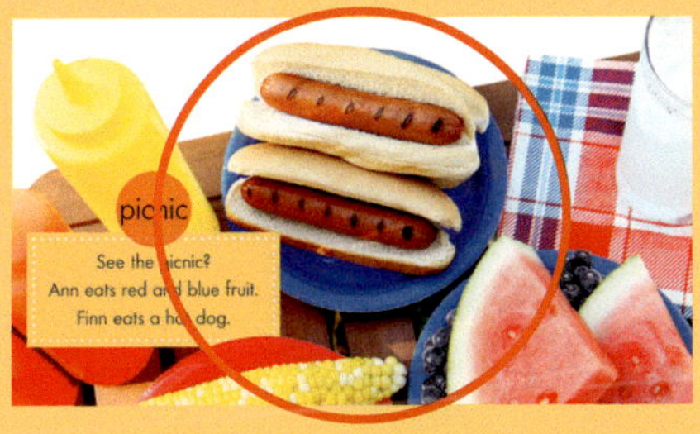

Spot is published by Amicus and Amicus Ink
P.O. Box 227, Mankato, MN 56002
www.amicuspublishing.us

Library of Congress Cataloging-in-Publication Data
Names: Schuh, Mari C., 1975- author.
Title: Independence Day / by Mari Schuh.
Description: Mankato, MN : Amicus and Amicus Ink, [2022] | Series: Holidays | Includes bibliographical references and index. | Audience: Ages 4-7 | Audience: Grades K-1
Identifiers: LCCN 2019053098 (print) | LCCN 2019053099 (ebook) | ISBN 9781645491033 (library binding) | ISBN 9781681526706 (paperback) | ISBN 781645491453 (pdf)
Subjects: LCSH: Fourth of July—Juvenile literature. |. Fourth of July celebrations—Juvenile literature.
Classification: LCC E286 .S38 2022 (print) | LCC E286 (ebook) | DDC 394.2634—dc23
LC record available at https://lccn.loc.gov/2019053098
LC ebook record available at https://lccn.loc.gov/2019053099

Alissa Thielges, editor
Deb Miner, series designer
Catherine Berthiaume, book designer
Bridget Prehn, photo researcher

Photos by Shutterstock/Rose-Marie Henriksson cover, 16, Steve Bower 1, Joseph Sohm 3, In Green 8–9, racool_studio 11 (blueberries), Tom Wang 12–13, Monkey Business Images 14; Wikimedia Commons/US Capitol 4–5; Alamy/David Grossman 6–7; iStock/kirin_photo 10–11 (picnic table)